GO ~~F*CK~~, I MEAN, FIND YOURSELF.

THE WISDOM YOU NEED TO GET OFF YOUR ASS AND CREATE YOUR BEST SELF.

GLENN LUTZ

Adams Media
New York London Toronto Sydney New Delhi

DEDICATION

This book is dedicated to the journey.

Adams Media
An Imprint of Simon & Schuster, Inc.
57 Littlefield Street
Avon, Massachusetts 02322

First Adams Media hardcover edition September 2018

ADAMS MEDIA and colophon are trademarks of Simon & Schuster.

For information about special discounts for bulk purchases, please contact Simon & Schuster Special Sales at 1-866-506-1949 or business@simonandschuster.com.

The Simon & Schuster Speakers Bureau can bring authors to your live event. For more information or to book an event contact the Simon & Schuster Speakers Bureau at 1-866-248-3049 or visit our website at www.simonspeakers.com.

Interior design by Erin Alexander

Manufactured in the United States of America

10 9 8 7 6 5 4 3

Library of Congress Cataloging-in-Publication Data has been applied for.

ISBN 978-1-5072-0859-5
ISBN 978-1-5072-0860-1 (ebook)

INTRODUCTION

You know that little voice inside your head? The one that's constantly saying things like *You're not good enough. You can't do anything right. You're never going to get to where you need to be.* Well, with *Go F*ck, I Mean, Find Yourself.*, it's time to take control of your life and tackle that negativity. It's time to find the you you're really meant to be.

I can tell you from personal experience that it isn't easy. Maybe you're struggling with self-doubt, feeling uninspired, or just stuck in a rut. Or maybe you're dealing with depression, anxiety, and low self-esteem like I was. Either way, it's tough to let that shit go…especially when that little voice bullies you at every step. It's time to shift your outlook and accept that there are ups and downs in life. It's time to get off your ass and do better to be better.

You are a powerful being with a purpose. You have the power to take control of your life, stop believing the bullshit, and make life into whatever you need it to be. Read this book. Take the words on each page, make them your own, and teach that little voice who's the fucking boss.

YOU.
THE ANSWER IS YOU.

GO OUT.
FUCKING GET IT.

**STOP TRYING TO FUCK
WITH PEOPLE
YOU SHOULDN'T FUCK WITH
AND WHO DON'T
FUCK WITH YOU.
PEEP THE VIBES.**

BOW OUT OF NEGATIVE CONVERSATION. IT ONLY LOWERS YOUR VIBE.

KEEP STAGNANT PEEPS OUT OF YOUR CIRCLE.

STOP TALKING SHIT.
IT'S COUNTERPRODUCTIVE.

BE FUCKING KIND.

**LOVE YOUR ENEMIES;
YOU DON'T HAVE
TO LIKE THEM.**

YOU CAN WISH
SOMEONE WELL
AND KEEP THEM
OUT OF YOUR CIRCLE
AT THE SAME TIME.

NOBODY CAN MAKE YOU HAPPY OTHER THAN YOU.

THAT JOB YOU'RE WORKING?
THAT LIFE YOU'RE LIVING?
WAS THAT YOUR EXPECTATION OR SOMEONE ELSE'S?

**PEACE IS YOURS
AND YOURS ALONE.
IT ISN'T BASED
ON EXTERNAL SHIT.**

**IDENTITY:
IT DOESN'T START
WITH YOUR
ETHNICITY OR NATIONALITY;
IT STARTS WITH LOVE.**

**DON'T ENSLAVE YOURSELF
TO SMALL BOXES
AND LOW EXPECTATIONS.**

BEING GREAT STARTS WITH BEING YOU.

**ALLOW YOURSELF
TO BE FUCKING FREE.**

DON'T TALK YOURSELF OUT OF YOUR DREAMS.

**MEDIOCRITY
IS WACK
AS SHIT.**

VISUALIZE IT, THEN FUCKING REALIZE IT.

**THERE'S SO MUCH SHIT
YOU DON'T KNOW,
SO DON'T PRETEND
LIKE YOU DO.
STAY CURIOUS.**

**WHAT DO YOU
TALK ABOUT MORE,
YOUR PROBLEMS
OR YOUR GOALS?**

**SPEAK INTO EXISTENCE
THE SHIT
YOU WANT TO SEE
IN YOUR LIFE.**

**IF YOU WANT
DIFFERENT SHIT
TO SHOW UP
IN YOUR LIFE,
YOU HAVE TO
THINK DIFFERENTLY.**

**BE OPEN
TO NEW SHIT.**

**GIVE YOUR INTUITION
THE RESPECT IT DESERVES.
TRUST IT.**

**STOP RESISTING CHANGE.
YOU NEVER KNOW
WHAT LIES AHEAD.**

**IF IT'S FOR YOU,
IT'LL FUCKING COME.**

**IF YOU GOT
WHAT YOU WANT,
RIGHT NOW,
WOULD YOU BE
READY FOR IT?**

FUCK FEAR.

A REDWOOD WAS ONCE A SEED.

SHAKE OFF
THE PAST BS.
EVEN TREES
LET GO OF OLD LEAVES
TO MAKE WAY
FOR THE NEW.

IS THERE ANOTHER
WAY OF LOOKING
AT YOUR PAST?
DID YOU MISS
THE MORAL OF THE STORY?

**DON'T ALLOW
YOUR NEGATIVE THOUGHTS
TO CONTROL YOU.**

IT'S ALL ABOUT YOUR PERSPECTIVE.

**SOMETIMES,
YOUR GREATEST LOSS
IS YOUR GREATEST GAIN.**

LET THAT SHIT GO.

FUCK HOLDING GRUDGES.

BITTERNESS SUCKS.

**EVER TRY MEDITATING?
SHIT HELPS.**

PUSH YOUR VIBRATION TO A HIGHER FREQUENCY.

**LOVE,
LOVE,
LOVE.
THEN LOVE SOME MORE.**

LOVE AS A STATE OF BEING, RATHER THAN AN EMOTION RESERVED FOR CERTAIN PEOPLE.

IF SOMEONE IS DOING SOMETHING ILL, LET THEM KNOW. HOLDING BACK COMPLIMENTS IS TOXIC AND LAME.

SHARE MORE.
DON'T BE A HOARDER.

GIVE BACK TO MOVE FORWARD.

GIVING > TAKING.

**YOU DON'T HAVE TO BE
A MILLIONAIRE
TO BE A PHILANTHROPIST.**

INVEST IN GOOD PEEPS.

**DON'T LET
ONES AND ZEROS
DETERMINE YOUR
SELF-WORTH.**

**IF YOU DECIDE
TO DO SOMETHING,
DON'T FUCKING COMPLAIN
WHILE YOU DO IT.**

WORK HARD AS FUCK.
PLAY HARD AS FUCK.

DON'T FUCKING GIVE UP.

**YOU'RE ALIVE RIGHT NOW.
YOU CAN STILL
ACCOMPLISH
ALL OF YOUR GOALS.**

YOU'RE GOING TO DIE; LIVE LIKE YOU KNOW THAT SHIT.

YOU WERE BORN
A FUCKING WINNER.
YOU LITERALLY WON
A RACE AGAINST MILLIONS.

**SPOIL YOURSELF.
CELEBRATE YOU.
YOU FUCKING DESERVE IT.**

WHEN WAS THE LAST TIME YOU GAVE YOURSELF A COMPLIMENT?

IF YOU DON'T BELIEVE YOU'RE THE SHIT, WHO WILL?

**MORE YOU,
LESS WHAT THEY'RE DOING.**

THERE'S ALWAYS SOMEONE
DOING "BETTER,"
AND THERE'S ALWAYS
SOMEONE
DOING "WORSE."
STOP FUCKING COMPARING.

HATERS WILL TRY TO RAIN ON YOUR PARADE. STAY WITH THE UMBRELLA.

**IT ISN'T YOU;
IT'S THEIR OWN
SELF-HATRED.**

BE SKEPTICAL OF THE SKEPTICS. BE CRITICAL OF THE CRITICS.

**HATERS GONNA HATE.
IT IS WHAT IT IS.**

STOP.

BREATHE.

BE FUCKING THANKFUL.

KEEP FUCKING PUSHING.

BEING STRONG IS DIFFERENT FROM LIVING IN DENIAL. DON'T PRETEND SHIT IS DIFFERENT WHEN IT ISN'T.

IF YOU'RE HURT,
LET YOURSELF HURT,
AND GIVE YOURSELF
TIME TO HEAL.
TREAT GRATITUDE
LIKE AN OINTMENT
FOR YOUR WOUNDS.

**DON'T PUSH
YOUR EMOTIONS ASIDE;
THEY'LL SHOVE YOU BACK
TWICE AS HARD
IN THE FUTURE.**

DON'T FEEL SORRY FOR YOURSELF UNLESS YOU WANT TO MANIFEST SORRY-ASS SHIT.

YOU'RE HUMAN.
SHIT HAPPENS.
ACCEPT IT
AND WATCH
YOURSELF GROW.

**THERE ARE SO
MANY FACTORS
WORKING AGAINST YOU;
DON'T BE ONE OF THEM.**

YOU'RE A CREATOR, CREATING ALL THE SHIT YOU SAY TO YOURSELF. SO LET'S BE MORE POSITIVE.

STEP UP TO THE FUCKING PLATE.

I AM (INSERT YOUR VISION HERE).

ENJOY THE FUCKING JOURNEY.

**YOU WON'T BE FULL
IF YOU'RE NOT GRATEFUL.**

GRATITUDE IS A DISCIPLINE. PRACTICE IT LIKE A SKILL YOU'RE LEARNING TO MASTER.

**VIEW GRATITUDE
LIKE A TELEPORTATION
DEVICE
TAKING YOU TO
THE NEXT STOP
ON YOUR JOURNEY.**

WHAT ARE YOU
THANKFUL FOR?

THE CRAP YOU BUY WON'T FILL THE VOID.

THAT FEELING YOU'RE LOOKING FOR WON'T BE FOUND IN MONEY. YOU HAVE TO LOOK INSIDE FOR FULFILLMENT.

ARE YOU INTO THAT
BECAUSE EVERYONE
ELSE IS
OR BECAUSE YOU ARE?

EVERYTHING GOES OUT OF STYLE. INVEST IN SHIT THAT LASTS.

**EVERYONE IS DOING
THE SAME FUCKING THING.
DON'T BE LIKE
EVERYONE ELSE.**

WHAT'S THE POINT OF BLENDING IN? WHY ARE YOU HIDING IN THE CROWD?

**THINK FOR
YOUR FUCKING SELF.**

PERSONAL ANCHORS: KEEPING YOU GROUNDED OR HOLDING YOU DOWN?

DO THE RIGHT THING. YOU'LL SLEEP BETTER.

LYING, CHEATING, AND STEALING? BAD FOR YOUR FUCKING HEALTH.

KARMA,
IT'S FUCKING REAL.

WORD IS BOND.
DON'T BE FAKE.
DON'T BE BULLSHITTIN'.

BE HONEST.
KEEP IT 100.

YOU'RE YEARNING FOR MEANING, RIGHT? SO FUCKING LIVE LIKE IT.

**FUCK MULTITASKING.
IF IT MATTERS,
GIVE IT YOUR
UNDIVIDED ATTENTION.**

**SHIT TAKES TIME.
MAKE CHOICES
THAT SUPPORT THE VISION.**

"LIVING" A LIFE,
NOT DOING
WHAT YOU'RE
SUPPOSED TO
BE DOING,
IS DEATH.
WHY DIE TWICE?

BE YOUR BEST SELF TODAY; DON'T WAIT FOR TOMORROW. THAT SHIT AIN'T GUARANTEED.

DON'T FUCK AROUND AND BE A LAMPSHADE TO YOUR OWN LIGHT.

**LOOKING FOR A WAY
TO REINVENT YOURSELF?
DON'T BE AFRAID
TO "SWITCH UP."**

IF YOU WANT DIFFERENT, YOU MUST:
THINK DIFFERENT.
SPEAK DIFFERENT.
BE DIFFERENT.

**DON'T BELIEVE THE LIES
PEOPLE FEEL ABOUT
THEMSELVES
AND PROJECT ONTO YOU.**

**DON'T WASTE
YOUR FUCKING TIME.
IT'S PRECIOUS.**

DON'T FEAR AGING; IT'S HAPPENING.

**DON'T USE EXCLAMATION
POINTS
WHEN YOU AREN'T
EXCITED.
BE TRUE
TO YOUR FUCKING
EMOTIONS.**

**DON'T FORGET,
TAKE OUT THE TRASH.**

DON'T LOSE YOURSELF FUCKING AROUND PLEASING EVERYONE ELSE.

LIVING FOR PEOPLE'S PRAISE AND ADMIRATION IS FOOLISH AND DESTRUCTIVE.

**STOP BEING CONCERNED
WITH PEOPLE
LIKING OR DISLIKING YOU.**

**PEOPLE WILL TALK SHIT
ABOUT YOU
TO FEEL BETTER
ABOUT THE PAIN
IN THEIR OWN LIVES.**

DON'T PUT YOUR INSECURITIES ON OTHER PEOPLE'S WORDS. WHAT DID THEY ACTUALLY SAY?

**AUTHENTICITY >
WHAT PEOPLE THINK.**

KEEP YOUR FUCKING HEAD UP.

KEEP YOUR EYES ON THE FUCKING PRIZE.

KEEP FUCKING GOING.

**ALWAYS STRIVE TO BE #1.
#2 AIN'T SHIT.
ACTUALLY, IT IS SHIT.
WE LITERALLY REFER
TO SHIT AS #2.**

LET THE BULLSHIT
PREP YOU FOR
YOUR SUCCESS.

DON'T BE CONTROLLED BY ANGER. YOU'RE POISONING YOURSELF.

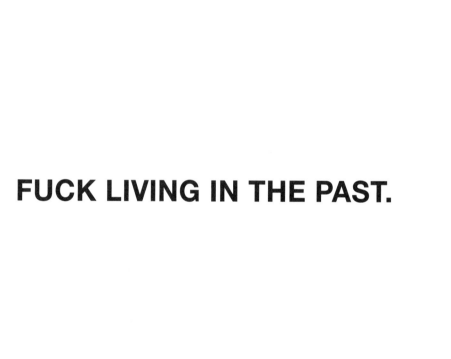

FUCK HAVING A VICTIM MIND-SET.

**TREAT PAIN
LIKE A DIVING BOARD;
JUMP INTO A BETTER YOU.**

DON'T LET YOUR PAST PUT YOUR FUTURE IN A HEADLOCK.

**ALWAYS FORGIVE.
IT'S THE KEY
TO YOUR FREEDOM.**

BREATHE.
DRINK SOME WATER.
IT'S ALL GOOD.

**TAKE CARE
OF WHAT YOU CAN.
LET WHAT YOU CAN'T
TAKE CARE OF ITSELF.**

THE UNIVERSE IS WORKING IN YOUR FAVOR.
GET OUT OF ITS WAY.

WE ALL WANT
TO BE LOVED;
WE ALL WANT TO
BE ENOUGH.
SO SHOW LOVE TODAY,
AND LET SOMEONE KNOW
THEY'RE ENOUGH.

**ASK SOMEONE
ABOUT THEIR DREAMS,
AND LISTEN.**

LISTENING > TALKING.

EVERYONE IS GOING THROUGH SOME SHIT. BE EMPATHETIC. STAY COMPASSIONATE.

STOP TALKING SO MUCH ABOUT WHAT YOU FINNA DO. GET LIKE NIKE AND JUST FUCKING DO IT.

SCARED?
THAT'S COOL.
NOW BE COURAGEOUS.

FORGIVE YOURSELF WHEN YOU MAKE MISTAKES. DON'T BEAT YOURSELF UP FOR BEING A HUMAN.

**WE ALL TRIP;
WE ALL SLIP.
SUCCESS IS GETTING UP
EVERY TIME.**

WHAT DO YOU SEE WHEN YOU LOOK IN THE MIRROR?

**SOMETIMES,
ACHIEVING BEAUTY
IS A PAINFUL JOURNEY.
EVER SEEN
A BALLERINA'S FEET?**

**LOVE YOURSELF
A LITTLE BIT MORE TODAY.**

REAL LOVE
REQUIRES REAL
VULNERABILITY.

REAL SHIT?
BE YOU.
NO ONE ELSE CAN.

IF NOT YOU, WHO?

WILL THE SHIT YOU'RE FINNA DO TODAY MATTER WHEN YOU'RE ON YOUR DEATHBED?

LIVE IN THE FUCKING MOMENT.

**BE PRESENT
FOR THE BEAUTY
LIFE THROWS AT YOU.**

**PICK UP
ON THE LESSONS
YOU'RE TAUGHT ON
THE JOURNEY.
DON'T HAVE TO BE
TAUGHT TWICE.**

BE AT PEACE
WITH YOUR PAST.

DON'T ALLOW NEGATIVITY TO HAVE A STRONGHOLD IN YOUR LIFE.

THROW AWAY THE QUESTION "WHY ME?"

IT'LL ALL MAKE SENSE IN THE END.

WHEN YOU GET
WHERE YOU'RE GOING,
DON'T BE AN ASSHOLE.
HELP THE NEXT
PERSON IN LINE.

GET OFF YOUR ASS.
CREATE YOURSELF.

YOU'RE AN ARCHITECT,
DESIGNING YOURSELF
WITH EVERY ACTION
YOU TAKE.
BUILD SOMETHING DOPE.

TAKE THE COURAGEOUS STEP INTO THE NEW YOU.

STOP LOOKING EVERYWHERE ELSE TO FIND THE ANSWERS.

YOU.
THE ANSWER IS YOU.

ACKNOWLEDGMENTS

I am grateful for the love and guidance I received at the hands of my beautiful parents, Rev. Stephen and Marlene Lutz, and my sister, Dr. Kathleen St. Louis Caliento. Thanks also to Steven Reneau for inspiring positive change and a redirection in my career; to Courtney Teagle for your friendship, character, and sound advice; and to Lauren Kimble for your wisdom and companionship. Last but not least, thank you to Khelsea Purvis for your generosity, editorial discernment, and for seeing and believing in the vision for this book; words cannot express how grateful I am for you.

ABOUT THE AUTHOR

Author Photograph by Devin Timothy Nelson

Glenn Lutz is an American author, conceptual artist, and poet, born to a Haitian mother and German father. His writings are centered on exploring the mind, and his work takes on an honest examination of relationships among identity, race, spirituality, mental health, and human nature. He currently lives in Los Angeles. You can find Glenn on *Instagram* at @glenn_lutz and his website, GlennLutz.com.